S0-AWN-486

A·MCMLXXVII

C · · M

SCVOLA SVPERIORE D'ARTE
APPLICATA ALL'INDVSTRIA

F.C. INTERNAZIONALE S.p.A.

Da Noi non funziona nulla (niente),
Però siamo tutti molto simpatici !!
(Emilio will make the translation)
With simpaty (for the devil)

Umberto Fiume

© 1984 - MAGNUS EDIZIONI SPA, UDINE

All rights of reproduction, in whole or in part,
of the text or the illustrations, are reserved throughout
the world.

Printed in Italy.

ISBN 88-7057-038-X

Invitation to Milan

Photographs
Mario De Biasi

Text
Luigi Barzini

Comments on the illustrations
Guido Gerosa

Translated by
Peter Lauritzen

Magnus Edizioni

This essay on Milan is the last text written by Luigi Barzini, junior. It was late November last year when it was decided to ask it of him. For a number of reasons, I could not meet with him until mid-January. We talked by the fire in his study. After recalling our many country walks and the fox-hunting we enjoyed together, I hazarded the proposal. «I would not ask it of you if you did not feel Milan the way few others do». Barzini looked at me steadily and answered, «Next week I go to Milan for a series of appointments with the doctors and then I am going to the Grenadines. I shall be leaving at the end of February, but you'll have your text before then». He never left for the Grenadines where, for a few months of the year, he used to seek a milder climate. As his daughter, Ludina, has recounted so well, it was in Milan that he first heard his sentence.

From that day on, with the courage that many, even close friends, mistook for presumption or the seeking after an effect, and which was really only his pleasure in the beau geste *(although bringing it off took guts), he would say with a smile for anyone who went to see him, «I have a tumour», adding that in a couple of weeks, he would be dead. After that he would observe the reaction of his embarassed guest. I thought that, as ill as he was and with so much to do, he would never have written a line about Milan. But I was wrong. Almost as soon as he came back from Rome, he set to work. At the end of February, his secretary rang to say that she had sent off the text. It reached me on March 16. Fifteen days later, the 31ˢᵗ, Barzini, who had heard the doctors' diagnosis exactly two months earlier, died. It was in the span of those eight or nine weeks that, in spite of his illness and his last committments, those unavoidable obligations before death, Barzini wrote these extraordinarily beautiful pages. It is quite clear that he chose to dedicate the little time that remained to him and his last efforts to Milan. Born in Milan on December 21, 1908 Barzini concluded his life writing about Milan. In this essay he wrote that above all the Milanese enjoy working. True enough. He worked right up to the last day.*

Corrado Pizzinelli

At the beginning of the twentieth century Milan was a busy, yet serious and dignified city. And it was still beautiful. There were few of the new streets, designed by Italian architects for South American cities or recalling Berlin, made by arrogantly disemboweling older quarters to accomodate a new industrial prosperity. Instead there were still the vast palaces and villas that preserved the city's late eighteenth century Neo-classical style: the courtly style of the Empress Maria Teresa, of Napoleon, of Eugene de Beauharnais and of the Archduke Rainer. Austrians, Frenchmen and the Austrians again, succeeded one another through decades of revolution and warfare without a perceptible alteration in the official architectural style. Scattered here and there were still many rococo palaces of the nobility, famous churches and a tangle of older, twisted littles streets that went back to the Renaissance or to the Middle Ages bearing curious names: the names of artisans like *Speronari* and *Spadari*, the spur and sword makers' streets. The circuit of the old city walls accompanied by its moat, the Naviglio, overlooked by antiquated gardens that trailed green tresses in the green waters. Frenetic modernism was represented by quick, jangling bicycles; by yellow trams and red taxicabs (both later painted a uniform green colour on Mussolini's orders); and by tall, shiny black automobiles ornamented with snaking brass klaxons and containing precious ladies dressed in furs fastened with posies of Parma violets; by public broughams or the private carriages which could be picked out by the shape of the coachman's top hat, decorated with a black leather cockade on one side, and by that of his whip whose thong was attached by a graceful curve and not joined by the sharp angle common to the others. Ladies went about their morning errands in carriages that halted here and there in front of famous shops. There were still many more donkey carts than lorries in the streets before the First World War and in the summer, the jolly snapping sound of the carter's whip, as loud as a fire cracker, came in at the open windows.

Then the world of industry began to predominate over that of the old aristocracy. Many of the nobles had been pro-Austrian and were still profoundly Catholic. They felt themselves more bound to the Royal Family than to the idea of the newly united Italy. The old, mustachioed king, living in the villa of the viceroys at Monza, had been invited, at first with a certain suspiciousness and then with greater enthusiasm, to the private balls given by the great families. Here and there in shady courtyards, commemorative plaques were erected to record his august presence at some mundane festivity. However, the nobles were interested primarily in land: in their own land. Like the people, they spoke almost always in dialect. Theirs was a sharpened dialect: ceremonious, precise and pronouneed with a French r; that of the masses was rounded, jovial and boisterous. The nobles and the peasants were the only ones who understood the complicated rules and ancient rituals associated with their prosperous agriculture: the times and paths followed by the water flow through canals to irrigate the water-meadows or fill the rice paddies or to water the pastures of the dairy cattle. They understood the obscure laws that governed the ownership of waterways, gullies, irrigation ditches and canals. The betrothed frequently brought their husbands a dowry that included, not only a box at La Scala and sundry other valuables, but also entire canal systems of cold runnig water. Many well-known noblemen, whose lack of an ancient title was compensated by a fortune made in silk or by tax collecting in the eighteenth century or by military contracting under Napoleon, despised the industrialists. They begrudged them their new wealth and their informal ways yet they occasionally conceded these new men their daughters as brides. These young ladies, considered acceptable even with a modest dowry, would bring refined usage to the new houses and would raise their children in a proper manner. The nobles of the oldest traditions, on the other hand, allowed their devotion to the old Holy Roman Empire and its antiquated usages to dim without embarassment, almost without noticing. They stilll took the waters at Bad Gastein or Karlsbad or at Marienbad instead of at Montecatini or Salsomaggiore. They went shooting in Hungary or in Croatia and Rumania. Their shirts and their cravats; their Virginia cigars; their courtesies and the manner in which they paid court to the ladies;

the coffee they drank; even their appearance still had something Viennese about it. Like all the aristocracy of Europe, they spoke French as a second language and they almost always spoke it well, aided as they were by their pronunciation of the *r*.

The early industrialists, almost all cotton manufacturers, held the true power in their hands. They were very serious, almost funereal gentlemen. They had money, the banks, the great *Corriere della Sera* newspaper, political and moral authority as well as worldly prestige. Their experience and their factory machinery came from Switzeland and from England. Almost all of them spoke English, the language of their religion. They knew it just as a priest knows Latin and just as the foreign clergy goes to Rome, they visited England often, going to Lancashire for business and to London for pleasure. They dressed in the English fashion and made their purchases at *Bellini's English Goods* in the *Galleria*, a shop surmounted, until only a short time ago, by a large, gilded British coat-of-arms. The materials and the models for their clothing were supplied by Prandoni, an excellent tailor who had studied cutting in London and had worked there at the end of the last century. His rooms, over the entrance to the Teatro Manzoni, were hung with autographed portraits of English lords in red hunting coats as if to assure his clients that they would emerge from his shop with an English air about them. The *Corriere's* editor, Albertini, was dressed by Prandoni as was the paper's administrator,

Eugenio Balzan; the editor insisted that all the staff use his tailor.

The cotton magnates considered the *art nouveau* style of interior decoration known as «Liberty» frivolous and untraditional and had their houses done in the more decorous fashion of hard, straight lines and light coloured veneers which they called *le style anglais*. Their households were run by impeccable English butlers who never uttered (the servants of the aristocracy were friendly, familiar and loquacious); hunting or racing prints hung on the walls; they took tea, always pouring a drop of cold milk into the cup first; they used beautiful writing paper with the address engraved in the corner in the fashion of Bond Street; they kept fifty-year-old collections of the *Illustrated London News* and *Punch*. Right up to the time of the sanctions imposed against Mussolini's Italy by Great Britain in 1935, Beppino de Montel (who was not in cotton, but in the equally important silk business), the owner of a racing stable (and what could be more English than thoroughbred horses?), president of the *Clubino*, a man who had enjoyed the costly favours of La Belle Otero, sent his shirts to London to be ironed just like the Dandies of the Second Empire.

The English alone were famous for giving starched shirts that flexible rigidity and that opaque surface that were considered indispensable. The cotton manufacturers were mostly liberals in the fashion of Albertini, that is to say, conservatives cautiously open to the innovations of the new century.

Commerce, a few banks and the newer industries were in the hands of little-known people who were beginning, with tenacity, to make their way. There were a few names familiar already: the Bocconi brothers, *Ingegnere* Pirelli, the Borlettis and the Falcks. These people came, for the most part from the provinces or from around the Lakes where the very first water-powered industries were born. These were the industries behind great new banks like the *Commercial* which was a German enterprise in the hands of Toeplitz and Goldschmidt. In fact many of these new industrialists spoke German: not the soft Austrian still familiar to a few nobles, but the hard, technical language of the Kaiser's Germany or else the peasant tongue of Switzerland. A number of them had studied precision tooling, commerce and finance in the Rhineland and the Palatinate or engineering in Zurich. The newer enterprises and commercial organizations employed a great number of German technicians and managers.

Many of the shops selling sanitary appliances and household goods or musical instruments were German. There were German chemists and the most famous sausage merchant in the city came from Prague. The young Milanese who studied in Switzerland or Germany acquired habits of an agressive rigidity and a scrupulous punctuality that made them hard bargainers in business. In turn, they put their children, as soon as it was possible, into the hands of German governesses who, until 1914, were still numerous. Curiously Milan's household gas industry was French. Pompously styled the *Union des Gaz Universelle*, it sent its bill collectors on their rounds in the flat visored cap worn by the Infranty of the Third Republic. The world of the intellectuals, writers, journalists and playwrights was French, too. They spoke to each other in the third person plural form borrowed from French novels and plays. America was represented by two or three cotton brokerage houses who furnished the industry with raw material, and by two dentists. The dental arts and cotton from the South were the relatively modest fields in which, at that time, the United States predominated: America was still in many ways a backwaed country.

At the beginning of the century, Milan still appeared an old European city, a city of small industry, of merchants, craftsmen and financiers. Old houses, antiquated streets, old-fashioned façades and ancient churches; villas reflected in their lakes surrounded by parkland and a hundred secret gardens in the heart of the city; antique hotels that had known Stendhal; La Scala; restaurants gleaming with brass and upholstered in velvet (one bore the name Hagy, an Egyptian pastry chef who had come to Milan from Alexandria with Napoleon); the affable honesty of the city's gentlemen; the amiable and ingenious spirit of the populace; good cooking; shining horses and light carriages; hospitable houses. All this made Milan a city of comings and goings, yet still placid, elegant, prosperous, cultured and civil. The smoky industries were on the outskirts. The Berlin style boulevards or South American *avenidas* were few. The business men hungry for success were scarcely noticeable, living as they did in new houses in new quarters set apart. Social unrest murmured secretly like an underground current emerging only in moments of crisis when sensible men lowered their newspapers, removed their pince nez and asked with agitated gestures, «But where will it all end? The world's going to the dogs!».

Senior members of the *Unione*, the city's oldest club, no longer felt secure. Every once in a while, they could hear from their windows the distant and muffled cries of upheaval, the bugle call ordered by the police commissioner, in bowler hat and tricolour sash, to disperse an illegal assembly and the hooves of the cavalry patrol sent to clear the streets. The noble lords of lands, villas and palaces, along with the cotton magnates and bankers; the big businessmen and the industialists in chemicals, steel and machine tooling asked themselves who could be inciting the masses, people who, left to themselves, were still devoted to the Church and the Royal Family; faithful to their patron Saint Ambrose; respectful of both old and new wealth; attached to tradition; good workers (like, for that matter, both the middle and upper classes); and always ready to remove their hats to a handsome equipage or in the presence of authority. The rich asked themselves why it needed only a few ruffians to intoxicate the people, make them forget prudence and the law and bring them to the Piazza to stand against the charges of cavalry as they had, in 1898, braved the cannons fired to disperse them.

It was known who these agitators were because they did nothing to hide themselves. They were hack writers, insignificant lawyers, hungry journalists, members of parliament, politicians appearing from heaven knew where, unshaven and sporting flowing black cravats, large floppy hats and had their heads full of a lot of disorderly ideas. They called themselves radicals, democrats, positivists, socialists, progressives, freemasons, materialists, atheists. They printed news sheets and published scientifc tracts on Darwinism or translations from fictional works about revolution. They organized cooperatives, leagues of mutual assistance and also labour unions. There were those who lived with Russian nihilist mistresses like Turati with Anna Kulischoff or later, like Mussolini with Angelica Balabnoff. There were even priests disappointed in the newly secular Italy: crazy priests whom the Archbishop in other times under the Austrian regime would have suspended or excommunicated without delay and denounced to the civil authorities but who now, in the atmosphere of spiritual confusion following the storming of Rome's Porta Pia gate, escaped his attention altogether. Despite the fact that these inexplicable upheavals reinforced the unity of the upper classes, the aristocracy, the cotton manufactures and the new industrialists remained suspicious in their dealings with one another. The nobles were irritated to discover that, little by little, industrial wealth was surpassing their own by a long way. The seasoned industrialists, those of the second and third generation, refused to believe that the impudent middle classes, an agressive bourgeoisie that made money in any conceivable way, could last for long. For example, they laughed at the Bocconi brothers for opening an immense store in the via Santa Radegonda where you could buy ready made clothing on many floors: they were said to be dealing in a janitor's rag trade. They laughed, too, at the Pirellis for manufacturing rubber heels. They all continued to lead their clearly separate lives, exchanging cold greetings in the street. They never received one another in their houses. It was almost as if one only needed to shut the gates, adjust one's civilities or eliminate a few names from the guest list in order to divert the course of History. However, they did observe each other with attention and curiosity. The newly rich indulged in servile imitations of the habits, manners and tastes of the older order while attempting to infiltrate slowly into the upper reaches of the social order. The state public schools provided one point of contact where the young could fraternize. The English-type boarding school where the upper classes perpetuated their superiority through offspring surrounded by school mates all their lives, found no favour in Milan – nor in the rest of Italy for that matter. It was in business where everyone,

regardless of the origins of buyer, seller, or financier, was pitted against one another. There were also the marriages which, little by little, linked new wealth with old, nobles with bourgeoisie in such a way that the off- spring freequently combined the qualities and defects of both. After all didn't Don Giuseppe Visconti, Duke of Grazzano, marry an Erba, the chemist's grand-daughter? The storm of the First World War arrrived unexpectedly. In the months of Italy's neutrality, many of the aristocracy, the conservative bourgeoisie as well as ardent Catholics of the middle and lower-middle classes – not to mention a large portion of the populace (virtually the same who had taken no part in the anti-Austrian uprisings of 1848) – favoured either the Triple Alliance or, at the very least, a policy of non-intervention. There were those who feared any war, not trusting the solidity of the newly unified Italy. There were those who remained faithful, if not to the Austrian Emperor himself – he was, after all, the same man who had fought to retain Lombardy in 1859 – at least to the idea of an authoritarian and hierarchical government as the best way to defend the traditional values of God and Country; the Family, Religion and Private Property without which society would collapse and life would have no meaning. The anglophile, liberal cotton manufacturers, like the more up-to-date factions of the aristocracy, were in favour of intervention. They were for the King and for the New Italy as a Mediterranean Power. They were

for the poet-patriot Gabriele d'Annunzio, for England and for the young Prince of Wales (later the Duke of Windsor) who hastened to the Front in the olive drab uniform of his soldiers. Many of the newer industrialists were in favour of a war that alone could give Italy its place among the great industrial powers of Europe. The radicals, the lawyers with their floppy black ties, and many intellectuals were for Italy's Latin sister-state, France, and for the «sacred principles» of Democracy that were being defended in the fields of Flanders. There were many fanatical socialists with them, too: often for confused and sentimental reasons. Others hoped to see the conflict transform itself into a truly world-wide conflagration followed by a universal proletarian revolution. But the most serious and responsable socialists were for neutrality and for universal peace. They found themselves fighting alongside the older-Austrians and Catholics with their differing ideals, just as, together, they had fought against the Unification of Italy from 1860 onwards and against the industrialists and their liberal civilization. All dissension was silenced after May 1915. All classes of Milanese fought with discipline and sacrifice. The city gave large quantities of money and of human life. Its industries contributed to the war effort in a decisive manner and many Milanese made their fortunes in these very same years. Then came Fascism and one could no longer comprehend anything. Virtually everyone dressed in the coarse woolen fabric favoured by the regime either from conviction, for discipline or to conform. The aristocrats, the cotton magnates, the industrialists, the radicals, the labour unions, the workers, the Catholics, the Socialists, the peasants, the poor all shouted the same slogans because Fascism assumed many forms and seemed the answer to each one's own particular anxieties. In the confusion of those twenty years, between one war and another, between one of the Duce's speeches and another, one great campaign or another waged to increase the production of corn or of children, the old divisions and the ancient processes of development continued under cover. However, none of these groups revealed its real identity, nor read its own newspapers, nor even had a clear conscience about what it wanted or would attempt to do. Economic self-sufficiency, the autarchy, had encouraged industries to spread around the outskirts, but it also encouraged the Milanese to remain passive in the presence of Roman arrogance. The official of Lombardy, once proud of their province's autonomy, adapted or pretended to adapt themselves to directives from above. They learned to take the overnight train to the Capital to see ministers and have the authorities resolve problems that, in the past, they themselves had solved alone. The old agrarian classes who produced rice, silk and milk hardly counted for anything any more, despite their ancient prestige and the glory of their names. Villas and palaces were falling into ruin and being sold to corporations or else were being divided into apartments and rented out. The new classes no longer attempted to imitate the manners and standards of the nobility. Many industrialists (especially those of the most recent vintage, the men of few traditions) were Fascists or else adapted themselves too easily to current trends. They would use Fascist protection for doing business, for amassing fortunes and for consolidating power. Beneath the identical uniforms, the differences between the various social classes became sharper. Perhaps that is the predominant characteristic of the period. The Milanese did not understand each other any longer. The only permissable rhetoric, the uniform rhetoric of the Regime, impeded any clear dialogue. Defended from Fascism, the old Milan, reactionary, Catholic, provincial Milan survived. The Duce had said that he wished to protect and develop the Milan of the 1906 Exposition. Thus an industrial and commercial Milan survived. The Milan of the unions and that of the proletariat, both bound to a sector of the Party and some of its internal movements, also survived. Yet secretly and quite unknown to one another, each of these groups also nurtured its own resistence to tyranny. Each formed a minority with its own inspirational ideals. Towards the end of the Second World War these groups joined a fraternal alliance united by their shared hatred. However, once Fascim had fallen, they had nothing more to bind them. One wanted the restored Church to predominate, another the return of the Constitutional Monarchy; some wanted a secular and democratic republic and others the triumph of Marxism and a dictatorship of the Proletariat.

What still united them all, just as it had done for centuries, was their passion for work. Milan is the only city in the world where the greeting, «*Buon lavoro!*» «Have a good day's work,» is repeated daily. In the most turbulant moments of history when no one knows what is happening, Milanese of all classes will throw themselves into work, forgetting reality, bitterness and fear. Take note that it is Work and not gain that is their passion. New industries are founded; the old are enlarged; sales are organized on a world-wide scale; great financial cartels are created. Milanese work has saved Italy twice in its history. The first time came after 1870 when the capital accumulated penny by penny during the eighteenth and nineteenth centuries in grain, rice, silk, milk, tariffs and trade served to finance the modernization of the peninsula, the construction of the railways, the rebuilding of Rome and the development of basic industries. In another sense Milan had to defend a way of life in the old way. From the earliest times when the Spanish installed their first Viceroy in the city, the Milanese had learned how to appease their distant governors and win from them an attitude of benevolent non-interference. The Court in its capital beyond the mountains and the seas must not suspect what the Milanese were up to, nor should they interfere. Milan sent tributes and embassies. They staged enthusiastic demonstrations for the Viceroys, offering them festivities, gala spectacles and illuminated parchments. They corrupted their governors with praise and money. All this just to be able to look after their own affairs in whatever really counted: in work, in production, in the sound administration of private and public wealth, in the construction of factories and in the strengthening of family alliances. In the period after the Second World War, Milan treated the capital exactly as it had treated Rome under Fascism: exactly as it had always treated Vienna and Paris and Madrid.

*

This is how I have seen the city where I was born, in the course of my life. I have seen it transform itself from a prosperous agricultural town, proud of the cheese of its countryside and of the music of its theatre, of its splendid palaces and churches, into an industrial metropolis comparable to Dusseldorf or St. Louis, Missouri. In fifty years Milan has followed a course that took France and England almost two centuries to cover. It has done remarkable things. It has also suffered from an indigestion of history. From decade to decade, men, families and classes have had to adapt themselves to new responsabilities, tasks and ways of life. The city has had to digest unprecedented waves of immigration. It is an old story. The city was virtually founded by the descendents of immigrants, transplanted over two centuries.

However, up until 1924 these were people who came, a few at a time, from the valleys, from the lake region and from neighbouring provinces like the Veneto. Having been inspired by ideals similar to those of Milan they were easily assimilable.

The city's unexpected and monstruous growth, the increase in population and wealth, the incredible number of every sort of activity, endanger the very character of Milan. The new quarters, many of which were constructed in place of the old tortuous streets, are anonymous quarters. They are without character, made by an anonymous society by faceless corporations and no longer by individual men. The municipal administration itself is a bureaucracy derived from other Italian regions and incapable of adequately defending the needs of the city and its surroundings. There are signs, however, that Milan will survive. I mean that the ancient spirit of Milan will transform the outsiders into Milanese and will succeed, little by little, in making its requirements felt even in Rome. The inescapable fact is that work changes whoever lives in Milan. At every level the exigencies of a job well done oblige different men to adopt uniform ways of life. Cunning (so beloved of other Italians), intrigues, administrative disorder, accounts that do not balance and thus impede and delay production, dishonesty, excessive caution and a suspicious attitude of mind are hardly in harmony with the rhythm of machines, with a massive export volume and with daily technical progress. Work has made the Milanese what they are and will transform the immigrants into true Milanese.

Luigi Barzini

A window on Milan

It is the idea of Milan that meets the eye at first glance: the impalpable atmosphere of a solid and rational dream, so drenched and soaked in fog as to be intangible and poetic. These images were realized in various seasons. They capture the secret heart of Milan and render the atmosphere of this most paradoxical of Europe's cities with a lyric fidelity: its very style sometimes nineteenth century or American, romantic or futuristic. A grandiose panorama (photo 1) gets to the heart of the matter, taking in all that signifies Milan both in the heart of those that live there and in the eye of the curious tourist. The orderly parade of the Cathedral's spires sparkling in artificial light; the silhouette of the cusp supporting the splash of colour that is the *Madonnina;* a cavalcade of clouds emerging from the intense ochre sky and, at the limits of vision, that massive fortress of opulence, the Torre Velasca. And all around, exalted in a symphony of sea green, skyscrapers loom up: glass houses, headquarters buildings; along with the nineteenth century palaces of Rovani's and Marco Praga's Milan, living symbols of two perfectly intertwined worlds. From its stones and from the streets neat spider web; from the precise lay-out of the metropolis comes that mixture of solid bourgeois virtues and affectionate fantasy that makes the Milanese prototypes of Italy's « Scandinavian », the Northern European worker and intellectual. The images of this Introduction continually delve into the human habitat of this nordic Italian in order to explain his style of life. For example, the Central Railway Station taken from an unusual angle in the Via Sammartini. There has always been a lot of ironic commentary on a rail terminal that reproduces the Babylonian taste of the nineteen thirties. But the angle from which we see it here gives it a different function as a vital organ, as the very lungs of the city.

The endless panorama of houses that stretch towards the horizon seem to be the Station's progeny almost as if Milan were the living result of traffic and movement: a human melting pot produced in the pulsating arteries of its railhead. Such an image is a symbol of the river of life that for decades – especially during the nineteen sixties – overwhelmed Milan and transformed Italy into another America: the goal of immigrants from all over the country.

In these first photographs, the artist's work has dealt consistently with two aspects: the suggestion of a classical Milan, the ancient and crepuscular city caressed by the fog or else the futuristic triumph of a New York-Milan, bold and proud of its lights, the ribbon of its highways, the reflections from its skyscrapers.

The dream Milan, on the one hand, repeating the nineteenth century rhythms from the drawing rooms of *contessas* and patriots; the Milan of the archepiscopal palace housing those cardinal-saints, successors of St. Ambrose, whom the people imagined to be future popes; the Milan of the *vie boheme* and of subtle, richly humorous poets; the Milan of irony and the dialect, so alive in its eccentric and intelligent people.

But beside all this, the constant heartbeat of Europe and of the world can also be heard. An intense dialogue with the entire universe, which uses Milan as the perfect spokesman, takes place in those skyscrapers that De Biasi has photographed in an impelling, tense light almost as if to emphasize their splendid impersonality. Banks, heavy industry, economist potentates, influential corporations: Milan presents itself here more clearly than in any sociological essay. Real power is transformed into a vision in these precise images. Then, too, there is the Milan of a lyrical abandon: a dreaming Milan. The city of a crystalline atmosphere (photo 6) with the Pirelli building in the foreground and the two skyscrapers of the Piazza della Repubblica. On those days of absolute light, there is a rare view of the Grigne alpine battlements in the background. The mountain range dominating the landscape gives Milan back its primitive enchantment, the simplicity of another age. Even the symphony of houses, tiny in comparison with the towering skyscrapers, assumes an intimate and familiar dimension in that light.

In reality, Milan is many things together. It is a window open on the year 2000 as well as the dizzying measure of an industrious Japanese-style Italy of the most advanced sort. It is also a secret and poetic universe that has not changed much since Stendhal, lost in a labyrinth of streets, went mad with the joy of discovering its mysterious ways, or

since Ugo Foscolo, hiding behind a column in San Babila, spied with jealous rage on his mistresses as they passed, seated in their carriages next to their husbands. Milan is the most suprising and least known of cities. Its windows, courtyards, pavements, churches and the Naviglio canals reveal unimaginable pleasures along with disquieting embitterment. The discovery of Milan is an adventure of infinite magic.

And the city's charm emerges also from an unusual meeting at the beginning of the book: a meeting with the dragon that is the symbol of Milan. De Biasi pursues the image of the dragon throughout the centuries and photographs it in a thousand different poses. It is a symbol that has lived in tactile immediacy and in a festival of colours since the time of the Viscontis right up to the Alfa Romeo era.

The heart of the city

We encounter the face of the great city in the heart of Milan, in contact with those realities that define its secret life.

The exploration begins in the drawing room, the Galleria Vittorio Emanuele. Seen from below, its extraordinary dome glows in an intense blue light. Images of the great Gallery's life stand out: the lazy flow of the human river over its mosaic pavement; the glassed-in, Parisian style cafes; the little pink baloons soaring up and lapping against roof of this *bonboniere*; the splash of colour provided by the *Carabinieri* in their black uniforms with red striped trousers and white bandolier belts. The air of Milan blows a busy kindliness through it, the rhythm of a placid race.

The Gallery is an example of Milan's natural artistic temperament. The pavement is worked like a mosaic. It indulges its whims in the whorls of an harmonious geometry from which the movement of human ants detaches itself. In the wealth of all these elements, the Gallery, seen in its entirety (photo 15) expresses the dignity of a solid bourgeoisie always intent on growth and on an ideal of an even psychological cleanliness.

But is there no room for boundless fantasy, for pure colour in Milan? Sometimes, yes. During a holiday, circus elephants parade past in a Fellini-like saraband.

The pachiderms lift their weight from the pavement's mosaic patterns bestowing the faint thrill of a dream on the city, a taste of the distant Orient. They have given back the timelessness of the fairy tale. Milan needs these doses of a nebulous unreality. It is too solid, too concrete and sure of itself.

Even this city needs reassurance in the long run. Its crowds (photo 16) have the same sign of loneliness as those in any of today's cities. Milan is ruled by the cold logic of post-industrial society. But all of a sudden, the futurist, skyscraper metropolis plunges into the past with a Time Machine. Its Piazza del Duomo, the classic centre of village Milan, again becomes the fair ground of a medieval town. One afternoon De Biasi discovered a spectacle in the square in front of the Cathedral shot through with a shiver of fantasy: a contorsion of clowns capering to music, challenging the coldness of industrial society. The clowns are two Canadian tourists, performers who provide themselves with a trumpet and saxophone accompaniment. They have come from the great, solitary American plains to discover another, more varied solitude. It is Christmas time and the Milanese have brought a Christmas cake and champagne besides money to reward the cold pavement-artist for his art on the Piazza (photo 19).

There is something profound and secret, too, in the symbiosis between Milan and tourists. One sees them curled up at the foot of ancient stones. They seem to be a part of the very life of those monuments and of the population of statuary that surrounds them. Milan gives of itself, perhaps because it is not a showy place like Rome or Venice.

It attracts people inside. It succeeds in making them participate in its mysteries and repeat again in time its ancestral patterns. Here are a couple of tourists on the Cathedral doorstep, in the shadow of the columns, who quite unconciously have struck the pose of Hayez' famous painting *Il Bacio* (photo 21). Rain transforms Milan and infuses it with the sense of an unknown world. This view of the Piazza della Scala (photo 22) is nonetheless revealing. The flower bed, which the passerby misses because his eye is usually drawn to the traffic's turbulance, presents a feast of colour in a flowering garden. A typically depressing Milanese atmosphere of silent greyness pervades the air while the bright yellow flowers in front of the Palazzo Marino and Leonardo's monument (photo 23) are echoed in the piercing yellow colour of the taxicabs.

The Palazzo della Ragione (photo 24) is one of the places where one understands the heart of Milan. It is a centre of pulsating life, one of those places where one is aware of history's span. It was the fulcrum of Milanese life from the thirteenth to the eighteenth centuries. This magnificent Romanesque palace, also known as the *Broletto Nuovo*, originally rose isolated amid a quadrangle of ancient buildings. And in a niche, gallantly astride one of those slightly weary stallions that belong to the tradition of Milanese monumental statuary, there is the *Podestà* Oldrado da Tresseno. He is remembered as the «Builder», the prototype of the city's leaders, those solid, rational beings with their feet well on the ground: from Alberto da Giussano to Alessandro Manzoni to Raffaele

Mattioli. In the Piazza San Fidele we find a pensive Manzoni lit up by the lights of Palazzo Marino. His attitude is that of the Great Lombard: a cautions, solemn meditation mixing religion and practical science and setting him completely apart from that vague fantasy of other Italians.

Surprise: Milan also knows how to be opulent and Venetian in lavish gold. The Poldi Pezzoli Museum seems quite new in the fulgid sparkling of its rich vitrines (photos 26) while the Tiepolo hall in Palazzo Clerici is a triumph in solid gold (photo 27 and 28). Here one feels the splendour of Spanish Milan resonant with carriages on the cobbled paving, the glamourous uniforms, the multi-coloured sumptuousness of grand balls. Still it is the Japanese-style Milan of the year 2000 that steps forward to present itself only partly hidden by a cushion of white flowers. The foreground is dominated by Arnaldo Pomodoro's vertiginous sculpture «Great Disc».

Returning to the enigmatic Milan of the silent centuries. Here are the giant caryatids, the great «*Omenoni*», who give their name to the house where Leone Leoni, the sculptor of the Emperors Charles V and Philip II worked and lived. Look at the proud but resigned Faces of these *Omenoni*. They are Milanese, too, with that bitter shrewdness hidden under their bushy beards. We penetrate the secrets of the palaces.

Pigeons fly over the roofs of San Satiro, a tiny jewel set in the midst of houses at the beginning of the Via Torino. And that hand

(photo 33) that sticks out at the entrance to Manzoni's house to caress the fabulous knocker also seems to express the possessiveness, the assuredness, the aristocratic nature of Milan. A city emerges solidly from the imperiousness of the lions to be found inside and from the enchantment and strength of its palaces' Romanesque heads. There comes an increasing desire to live it all, to penetrate this endless city. Here, in an unusual panorama, is youth besieging the Brera courtyard (photo 38) and, in an astonishing sequence, the great symbols of modern life. Today, Milan is the centre of fashion, of taste and of elegance. The conquest of the world of imagination is expressed by maniquins dominating the great designers' windows in the smart shopping streets. Who would have ever said that Milan, so rational, so precise, so prosaic would also be the heartland of fantasy in clothing? But do not forget that this is also the land of Carlo Porta and Manzoni; of Gadda and of Marco Praga's great journalism; and of a bohemian style of life.

From the Montenapoleone to the secret courtyards and rare gardens, like the one behind the Archeological Museum in Corso Magenta, everything is a crescendo of discoveries. The Milanese draws on a magical atmosphere in his little Versailles, the Villa Comunale in Via Palestro (photo 43). The *Triennale's* upside-down angel (photo 45) seems the incarnation of an anti-conformist, ironic and fleeting Milanese fantasy.

Milan: a return to Romantic sighing in the

carriages lined up along the cloister in the *Museo della Scienza*. The shudder of adventure felt by the lonely heroes of modern capitalism can be experienced in the Piazza degli Affari and in the halls of the Stock Exchange where the vibrant air of the photographs expresses greed, the rapid movement of money and the uncertainty of success.

Milan is all this. And after having chased after fortune, it rests in airy cupolas, in the colourful garden serenity and in the massive power of the Sforza castle. Its secret heart has mysterious heartbeats and the inward power of the faces in the Rondanini *Pietà*. Towers, fortresses, luxurious dwellings, wealth and fantasy: from the dynasties of the Sforza and the Visconti to Manzoni and Stendhal; from the Banca Commerciale to Armani, Milan is the saga of a majestic heart of stone capable of trembling with human emotions.

10

11

13

14

17

18

19

20

21

22

24

26

27

31

33

34

35

39

40

41

45

47

51

53

55

56

The mountains of faith

De Biasi has selected three churches from a hundred possibilities to express Milan's religious spirit. Why three? Because the Cathedral is the symbol of the city and represents its identity. Sant'Ambrogio is the church of its patron saint and in the shadow of Santa Maria delle Grazie shines Leonardo da Vinci's *Last Supper*. There is a great wealth of churches and religious art in Milan, but this selection has sought to restrict the dialogue to the most intimate spiritual arguments. Here is the Cathedral in its most familiar guise (photo 59) at the beginning of the voyage into the churches. The authentic power and natural elegance of a gothic cathedral, resembling an oak tree sprung from the earth; the band of light from the *Madonnina;* and in the foreground, Victor Emanuel on horseback, a bit amazed by so much splendour. De Biasi introduces us to the lacy intricacy of the spires, a subtle embroidered construction, while the statuary population seems to be amusing itself at the expense of lost visitors. But the curious spirit of the Milanese is expressed in the singular point of view of photograph 61 - quite unusual. The wide angle lens turns the Duomo's roof into a Piazza crowded with tourists, the swarming centre of a village world. The metaphor of Milan as a village keeps presenting itself: an enormous fantacizing community that gathers itself together in a few symbolic places and displays its picturesque life as that of an indutrious tribe.
How many of the Milanese hurrying by have ever noticed the tender magnolia in photo 62 reaching out from the Piazza Campo Santo to caress the Duomo's white flanks.
De Biasi indulges in a poetic pilgrimage in search of the mysterious sources of being Milanese: the feeling that runs along the stoney statuary limbs, along the mosaic pavements or through a lovely sky when, in the Manzonian sense, it is fine.
We are hunting for unusual images with which to paint this anomalous city. A city whose secrets are not easy to penetrate. Here are the Duomo's statues (photo 63) framing that willful edifice, the Torre Velasca. Intertwined here are history and wealth; art and business; the potent spirit of the eternal and the suffocated shudder of the ephemeral. Milan is also the discovery of the interior of things. The Cathedral candelabra (photo 64), lost in a fever of restoration, has the impact of a futuristic object dispersed in a metaphysical city. Some details of the doors are terribly worn because people cannot resist caressing them with a superstitious abandon. The wounds inflicted by blind love are also evident in the shiny, fleshless limbs of bas reliefs.
The Cathedral evokes visions of popular fervour, of religious passion and of collective enthusiasm. In its stained glass, eternity is accompanied by a darting ironic smile, a caustic interpretation of humanity that makes one think of a Breugel or an Hieronymus Bosch (photo 67). Even here Milan lives in its own secret dimension between Carlo Porta's irony and the lyric transport of Manzoni's

Inni Sacri. The solemnity of Ambrosian catholicism appears in traditional painting, a world redolent of San Carlo and Federigo Borromeo and in the devotion expressed by votive candles placed before the gilded Madonna (photo 68). The photographer-artist's sensitivity synthesizes these emotions in a single image, an extraordinary symbol: the statue's haughty colloquium held against a background of luxurient, magical sunlight (photo 70).

At Santa Maria delle Grazie solemnity often gives way to a fabled lightness. In the cloister, the tenuous symphony of arches animates a highly enjoyable architectural movement. Frieze and statuary details display the supreme elegance of the whole. Visconti dragons, symbols of Milan, entwine in an embroidery of surrealist sinuousness. And another dialogue is added to the fantastic colloquium of the Duomo's statues: that of the Apostles in the *Last Supper*. It almost symbolizes Milan as the civilized city *par excellence* - a world of dialogue, of conversationalists, of intertwining personalities, all symbolized in the kaleidoscope of its art.

At Sant'Ambrogio one is struck by the eloquent bareness of the building and its walls, and by that air of sublime archaic nobility. Perhaps the most beautiful corner of Milan and that where one breathes an atmosphere of limitless classicism. Above all the sculptures there emanate a sensation of solid fantasy that brings their surroundings alive. Here are the hands of a statue (photo 81). They have the suppleness, the curiosity, the animation, the vitality of the Milanese world. And so we see, wandering in search of these monuments, that each line carved in stone, each detail, each marble vein describes Milan's mysteries and participates in a single enlivening reality.

De Biasi understands Milan as a landscape permeated by an inadvertent, silent melody of rain. Even Sant'Ambrogio appears unusual with the rain's reflections enlivening the stones (photo 82). A secret, subterranean city difficult to discover, Milan lives in the flickering rain, in the reflections of the lights and for the daring, unfamiliar glimpses, like that in photo 83, that conclude this exploration of the «out of the way» basilica. One begins to discover the city's characteristics in the landscape of these churches revisited: its shyness and extreme timidity, a coy reluctance to reveal its immense beauty save to those who have the strength to pursue it beyond the veils of appearance. This solid Milan appears simple and transparent while instead it lives by a hidden, poetic disdain. Only by plunging with abandon into the heart of its monuments, refusing the facile façade and discovering the acute dissatisfaction of the abnormal and unusual, can one distinguish the extraordinary fantasy of its world.

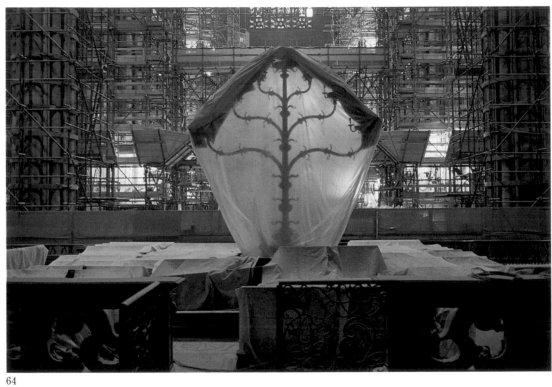

64

65

67

71

73

74

77

78

79

80

81

Façades and windows

Milan is not like other cities where quarters have a precise physiognomy: a Baroque quarter, a Renaissance one or an Art Nouveau one. The Lombard metropolis is characterized by its fantastic mixture of styles. One building of a certain type is followed in the same quarter by its diametric opposite. The result is an eclecticism of a surprising variety. One finds this out for oneself in the discovery of Milan's facades. Portrayed from below and with serpentine reflections in its facade, the Pirelli skyscraper (photo 84) is a futuristic vision. The symphony of its geometric glazing produces an abstract effect, a network of lines and volumes like a Mondrian painting.

The play of Milanese facades varies from classic linearity to a Florentine Renaissance taste for rusticated stonework; from the airy windows of Milan's eighteenth century and Imperial era to the lucid geometry of the ultramodern buildings. Even in this, the city's spirit requires a co-existece of styles and worlds which makes a distinctive feature of extreme variety.

The super rich reside further along the via Sant'Andrea in the very heart of Milan. This house with its blue shutters and discreet balconies (photo 85) gives an impression of aristocratic solidity. In Piazza Castello (photo 86) the severity of rustication and the play of wrought iron in the windows leave an impression of power. The Florentine style dominates the Foro Bonaparte (see also photo 88), this corner of Milan that has the spaciousness of parkland and the elaborate planning of a great nineteenth century city. Its patrician houses present a sparkling profile. The projecting windows are woven over with wrought iron, giving wing to the austere outline of arches and columns while describing a setting of Napoleonic and neo-classical grandeur. We have come back here to breathe the scent of Stendhal's inimitable Milan: the assonances of antique palaces, the subterranean fascination of forgotten courtyards and the strength of those windows decorated in iron.

Here we are yet again in the futurism of H. G. Wells' novels, a scene from the war of the worlds. Futuristic lace, so different from the Duomo's ornamentation, in a building on the Via Melchiorre Gioia (photo 89) expresses the daring of the year 2000: the science fiction adventures, the clones, robots and other magical creatures from tales about Mars. We never cease to be amazed. The Milan of facades offers clamorous example of the coexistence in this city of worlds separated from one another by light years. From mediaeval and Baroque examples down to the future Metropolis and on into the realms of pure fantasy.

Then we might as well give ourselves up to the play of the imagination in exploring, through the solitary cry of a finely wrought window, the sense of a buried civilization. Here we find ourselves in front of the window of the Palazzo Castiglione, an extraordinary example of Art Nouveau on the left side of the Corso Venezia, built by the architect Sommaruga in 1903.

Its highly theatrical staircase inside, its chiselled facade, and its bizarre windows establish a standard for Art Nouveau architecture in Milan. The richness of the whole is here extolled in its particulars. The enchantment of one of its windows (photo 91), a jewel-like slit, a port-hole opening into the mystery and anxiety of beauty. The play of iron bespeaks an Art Nouveau dream in the taste of Gabriele D'Annunzio, a morbidly senile return to the Middle Ages. Extremely beautiful, but pallid when confronted by the perfect Renaissance design of a window in the Castello Sforzesco (photo 92): exemplary in the balance of its volumes, the play of light and shadow and the restrained majesty of the whole. In this case, the infinitely solemn obtained with the infinitely sober. The handsome window of the Ospedale Maggiore (photo 93) with its pretensions to wealth respresents another more important thread. Curiously, Milan is an extremely serious society which loves the theatrical, amusements and illusionism, almost as if it were tempering its own rigidity. There are examples of playful windows, of theatrical facades and even a *tromp l'oeil* window set like a mirror in a palace wall (photo 96). Solemnity, grandeur, and majesty; levity and play. Few things furnish us with a better insight into Milan's complex soul than these windows. We are confronted by completely different styles and worlds. Here is the entrance to the Vittorio Emanuele Gallery from the Piazza del Duomo (photo 97): a magical stage setting and the mystical gulf with an entire orchestra set out behind it. On the other side of the building is the most disconcerting, luxuriant and sumptuous example of Milanese Art Nouveau: Milan's strangest facade with its amusing sculpture and mosaics (photo 98).

But here again is Mondrian's geometry in a palace of the Centro where a ray of sunshine extolls the facade's pure abstraction, chasing after pure rhythm, intertwining geometric fantasies from the new frontiers of future centuries. In her architecture, Milan reminds us that she is the laboratory of the future. We are almost overwhelmed by the imminence of other worlds, by the superimposition of images and historic proposals and memories. Infinitely affected fantasy turns into poetry in the whorls of painting and the iron balconies on Milan's most beautiful Art Nouveau house in the Via Malpighi (photo 99): a shudder of curiosity, an airy play of forms, a variety of architectonic smiles. And here again, the theatrical impetus on the facade of the Teatro Fossati in the Corso Garibaldi (photo 100). In its glory, this was the setting for many a Futurist evening as well as being a favourite haunt of Marinetti. The pretensions of an agrarian Milan present themselves as the dream of farming aristocrats, the enlightened realm of silent, efficient men, the great city with the Brianza countryside behind it like a soft mirage. It can be understood by looking at the facade of the Piazza Sant'Erasmo (photo 103): arcades, loggia and the front of the building, all buried under the veil of climbing vegetation. A perfect illusion of the country like the evasion offered by an eighteenth century Arcadia.

But almost immediately afterwards, we fall back into the future again. The dizzy sensation of futurism is evident in the pure masses of Milano Fiore, the metropolis of the year 2000. The artist of the lens has captured the sunset glow on a facade of the palazzo dei Congressi where the Milan Trade Fair will have its future headquarters. A flash of the immensity projecting into a science fiction future. Tomorrow's planet illuminates Milan's latest facades with its cruel hope.

85

86

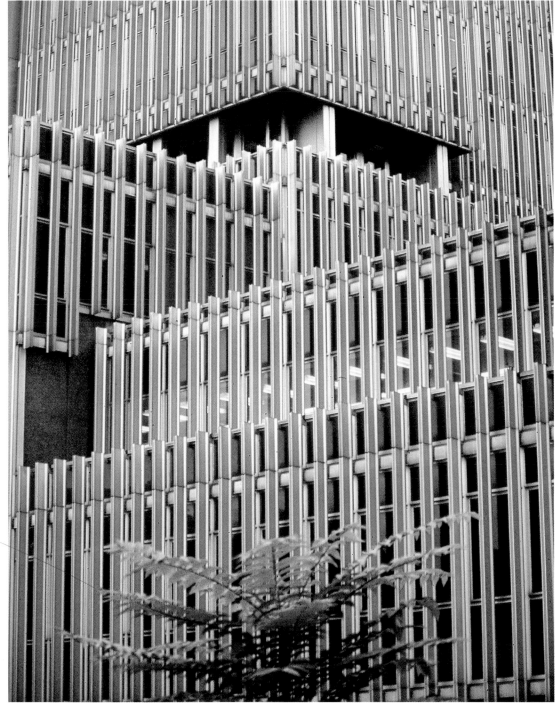

91

92

93

94

95

96

100

101

102

Inside the secret of the courtyards

In the course of this new stroll we shall discover the face of the most secret and hidden Milan. The often unsuspected courtyards represent a revelation of the soul of a profound city. They permit us to wander from the aristocratic world to that of the colourful variety of the people. Guided by De Biasi's eye, we enter not only into courtyards that cannot be seen from the street, but also into the little separate courts where a carpenter, heir of a long tradition, has his work bench and shop. We penetrate majestic palaces through solemn entrance halls and theatrical staircases, but we also explore the courtyards of the tenements: a nineteenth century world with the washing hung out to dry and people engaged in animated discourse from one window ledge to the next, endowing their daily life with the pace of a play.

We have reached the true heart of our discovery. The journey through the unknown metropolis becomes truly unusual. We penetrate into a secret Milan, a city that is discovered by walking tirelessly through its by-ways with out a guide. While Venice is a «visible» city, eloquent in its glory, here we must constantly set out to discover the poetic city's untold and veiled aspects. Photography is the best ally to extol this discovery. It permits the enlargement of detail and immersion into the meaning of things. As when the white spot of a nun's habit stands out against a background of University cloisters and greenery: the delicate touch which humanizes a rare, architectural elegance (photo 105). Entering a courtyard in the Corso Venezia is like a magic passage from *Alice in Wonderland:* well tended hedges and shrubs, the mosaic walk carressed by long shadows, a fabulous play of raking light (photo 106). The reverent wonder shown by the two girls on roller skates for a piece of sculpture at the Palazzo Bagatti Valsecchi in Via Santo Spirito (photo 108) humanizes the refined play of the beautiful paving, the balconies and the tall windows.

Milan is unpredictable: its whimsicality is a constant surprise. Take a glance at another courtyard in the Via Manzoni, that of Cardozzo's famous Naviglio Gallery (photo 108). A Rolls Royce stands next to a delivery van: glory and wealth are wed to daily life, to the everyday job. And this, too, is Milan: the city where the very rich awaken worried and rush off to work anxious not to lose their magic moment.

There is nothing more modest and yet more eloquent than these Milanese courtyards. A glance at that in the Corso Magenta 67 (photo 109) or the one in the Palazzo Borromeo in the Piazza Borromeo (photo 110) is sufficient to feel the limitless fantasy that permeates the arches and the walls; that invades the windows along with the light that flits over the faces of the antique statuary. Man is lost before the symphonic crescendo of colonnades, the pavements' burning colours, or in the solitary passage into the courtyard of a religious house in the Corso Venezia (photo 111). But discovery never ends: the wealth of colours and decoration in Milanese courtyards recalls the patios of Spanish houses of Mediterranean garden architecture. Visits become even more surprising: in Via Montenapoleone (photo 112) a courtyard is dominated by the shadow of palm trees and the lamplight spreading a reassuring atmosphere of nineteenth century enchantment. And here are other courtyards, even in Roman style: a fantasy of columns, capitals, heads and fragments of statuary in a classical climate heavy with evocation. In a courtyard in the Via Borgonuovo (photo 115) the greenery spreads its restful shade over one of Milan's many splendid gardens. The courtyard of a palace in the Piazza Sant'Alessandro, a masterpiece of Milanese Baroque (photo 113) is a miracle of harmony and elegance with its precise proportions, the vibrant hue of the walls, the reverberation of light from above and the shadows cast by the iron gates. A softness of lines that is repeated in a series of classic sites in the most exclusive part of Milan. Here is Palazzo Litta, a grandiose patrician residence from the city's sunniest age. It was built by Ricchino for Count Bartolomeo Arese and its interior has precious period rooms such as the eighteenth century *Sala degli Specchi*. But what one particularly enjoys on this walk is the limpid classic elegance of its courtyard with the purity of its colonnade. And here is *Le Stelline* (photo 119), one of the purest and most dazzling of Milan's courtyards, with a glimpse of Santa Maria delle Grazie nearby. It is a building devoted to light that breathes festivity and youth.

Today it is used primarily for conventions. In the Via Valpetrosa 5 (photo 120) there are two courtyards, one inside the other, and together they form a really theatrical scene. They seem a backdrop ready for a play. Milan never ceases to amaze. Here in a courtyard in te Via Carlo Maggi (photo 121) a carpenter is removing his plywood in the evening. The photographic eye has captured an extraordinary synthesis, giving a sense of the profundity of the surroundings and yet recreating the intimacy of a scene from Milan's nineteenth century. A series of roof tops, laundry hanging out to dry, iron bannisters, red tile roofs, mushrooming television antennaes: the variegated world of the Naviglio canals. Nature is wed to art and to life in Milan. Here is the courtyard of Pomodoro, the sculptor, in the Via Vigevano with his sculpture in the foreground (photo 123). And in the Via Col di Lana in the Ticino quarter, there is a world full of popular vitality where Milanese exuberence explodes in the tenement houses. The women at the window ledges (photo 124) and the rooftops follow on as picturesquely as in the Paris of René Clair's films. Milan is an overflowing fantasy, it is derision and desecration (photo 126). Enraged tenants in the Via Carlo Maggi have painted the doors of the house. The Big Eye is watching you, analyzing you, spying on you. It is a playful game as well as a warning. Recovering from this bout of mockery, here again is something grandly classical: Bramante's solemn cloister, a jewel of line

and proportions, seen from the bell tower of San Sempliciano (photo 126). Our exploration closes with the courtyard of the Catholic University. A jewel of jewels: an architecture of lacerating lyricism; of fantastic grace; impregnated with a sense of the eternal, musical and immersed in green. It is an ancient and yet youthful world with the poetry of being Milanese dripping from every pore.

109

110

112

113

114

115

116

117

Stone carpets

Frequently one has the world at one's feet without noticing. Harmless and widespread commonplaces teach us from childhood to keep our heads up; to reach for the stars and to keep our eyes fixed on the faces we meet. But hardly anyone thinks of bending down over the treasures that are spread out beneath us. Yet the pavement, either ruggedly bare or solemn, or else elegant or coy, is civilization's most faithful mirror. Anyone knows that who has walked the historic pavements of Paris or Vienna, of Prague or London for days on end.

Mario De Biasi has also applied his great qualities as an observor to Milan's pavements and has taken from them that same concrete poetry that is the characteristic of the city in its squares, churches and courtyards. The intelligent lens obliges us to look inside ourselves as well as around us. The curious passerby ends by discovering the reality of the world over which he walks by exercising a spirit of observation. He picks out the existence of treasures that he never before suspected or noticed.

Foro Bonaparte. The sonorous name of this noble Milanese avenue is reflected in the pavement's measured solidity: stones laid like the tesserae of mosaic; coloured like the frogging of a Napoleonic uniform; divided by tram tracks until they form the equivalent of a geometric artist's fantasy (photo 129). The photographer shuffles the length of Milan while precisely chiseled work reveals itself beneath his knowledgeable feet. Pavements all inlaid with subtly embroidered outlines and colours: the play is delicious and appears to move in a tapestry dimension. Whorls follow inlays; the network of the design becomes ever denser and more precise; the pedestrian moves as if through a wall of undulating illusion between the rich squares traced parallel in the heart of the earth. An unknown artist designed an elegant herring-bone pattern in this street paving (photo 133). Lichens have sprouted from the thin mildew accumulated over the years. Ever more curious fantasies nest in the pavement of the *Biblioteca Comunale* in the park (photo 134) or in that fabulous pavement at the *Stelline* (photo 135). Colours follow one another with an extraordinary joy. They compose festive visual symphonies of special vividness: reds, yellows, violets, blues, deep greens and orange. Tortuous masses, anxious or joyful according to mood, exclamatory like giants' clubs, delicate like the wind sighing over the fields. These surprising Milanese pavements recall famous graffiti: the large, coloured drawings, both abstract and figurative which Hippies used to decorate New York subway walls in the nineteen sixties. Here, too, in the pavements of Milan, just as in the American subway, there is an incredible proliferation of arabesques, crazy figures forming a spontaneous generation of dreams and nightmares.

This is, perhaps, the most remarkable aspect of the poetic joy of the metropolis. At certain times, it assumes an archeological dimension, almost as if one might discover these paving stones in some post-apocalyptic future and wonder at the narrative vitality they express. Strange animals and floral designs of every sort animate the floor of the Palazzo Bagatti Valsecchi (photo 136), while that of the church in the Corso Italia (photo 137) is bare and severe, almost emanating a wise warning from the other world.

The pavement in front of the church of San Sempliciano (photo 138) rises to the essential linearity of sculpture. It has an absolute purity of line and concedes nothing to loops and squiggles or to arabesques. It expresses a simple eloquence that is completely Milanese, a strong joy of living that is still modest and restrained, without any trimmings.

The great floor of the Gallery (photo 139) seems to illustrate the discovery of nature, a revelation of quartz, crystals, precious stones and rare elements. Two Milanese observed the photographer taking this picture and, from his appearance, mistook him for a foreigner. They talked about him in loud voices, laughing, convinced that he could not understand.

«Look at that, he's photographing the warning in the floor», said one of them. «How odd», the other answered, «we've passed here a thousand times without ever noticing it».

In reality the artistic eye is an acute and constant discovery. It explores and uncovers the significance of things where no one suspected them of being.

Finally, the highly exalted poetry of pavements in the poetic flooring of Corso Magenta 67 (photo 140). It has the geometric purity of a painting by Paul Klee. The Milanese walk daily on top of these fantasies and often never think about the treasure that lies buried beneath their heels. But the intensity which the city exudes, its well-disciplined feverishness, its quiet and intimate air, the overall fantasy of its design emerge irrepressibly even in the magic of the pavements. The lyricism of the pavement designs is continuously present and influences the surroundings in an extraordinary way, even if only few are aware of it.

130

131

132

The green islands

A widespread legend maintains that Milan has no greenery. The most general conception is of a city suffocated by cement with grey, oppressive barracks cluttering the outskirts and reaching out to strangle the historic centre with a degrading quality of life. But the lyric lens denies this vision of a pitiless Milan, as a metropolis without lungs. You must search, but eventually the vision of a sunny, wooded Milan discloses itself, a humid, growing city. The fantasy of its yearning parks opens itself to the passerby. A Milan-London and a Milan-Paris with bashful strolling lovers abandoning themselves gaily on the lawns while the band plays behind the trees; with a picnic; with the sun's eye happily blinking after having broken through the clouds.

Here is the park of the Castle. The tree's indistinct outline; leaves trembling; the timid suggestion of a kiss. Milan conspires in the dream with the humanity of its trees that stretch their leaves to greet love's miracle (photo 141). The London atmosphere multiplies (photo 142-143) during the holidays. All the trees are in flower; couples stretch out happily on the lawns; behind the white fog, familiar outlines stand out like the *Arco della Pace* and the *Teatro di Burri* whose white and black walls provide a backdrop for the scene. The lawns extol a human relationship. They permit us to attribute a particular tone to the sighing, to the rumblings, to the echoes of each word. And thus the city, surprised in its green silence, ends by acquiring a different appearance freer, far from the eternal cliché of the hyperactive, inhuman Milan.

Visions of other worlds emerge from the intertwining trees and undergrowth. The cupola of the observatory in Corso Venezia, «surprised» in an unusual position (photo 144), has the futurist magic of an image caught in Los Angeles. In the middle of these lawns, one is pursued by a suspicion of a Milan-California, by a city of the future firmly anchored to tradition but with astonishing openings. But there is also a continuous intellectual see-saw between the world of nineteenth century Bohemian romanticism and the futuristic world of science, technology and revealed marvels. The Lambro park (photo 145) provides an image of an eighteenth century Arcadia or the lakes of Wordsworth and Coleridge. The discovery of Milan's parks and gardens brings forth a romantic aspect with an almost forgotten sweetness. As Luciano Zeppegno says so very well in his *Alla scoperta di Milano sconosciuta*, «There is the gradual and stimulating, yet at the same time, irritating discovery of the surprising quantity, and of the even more surprising beauty of the private gardens, true oases that the natural privacy of the Milanese (especially the rich and discreet) succeeds in concealing quite well. In some streets, apparently closed off by brick and stone walls, just beyond an entranceway guarded by a surly *portiere* (Milanese doormen are almost always surly) and perhaps through one or two courtyards, truly beautiful and not always small, green spaces are hidden». From the dead leaves of a garden in the Via Circo emerge the *Discobolus'* powerful limbs (photo 146). An enigmatic head with penetrating eyes and mysteriously half-open lips pierces the tangle of vegetation in the courtyard of the Columbus Clinic (photo 147). Flowers, bushes, shrubs and trees compose a strange symphony of vegetation and dazzling play of colours in the famous garden at Corso Magenta 67 (photo 148) known as Leonardo da Vinci's vinyard. From there Leonardo would lean out and see the solemn outline of Santa Maria delle Grazie. These tales and legends compose the picture of an unknown Milan, a city of fantasy and of the tender poetic response, the green capital of the romanticists. The Spring play evoked by the trees in the Corso Magenta makes one think of a Botticellian «triumph» constructed by nature.

We return to limpid neo-classical surroundings in the gardens of the Villa Reale, a triumph of an ordered and well composed nature (photo 149). And here (photo 150) is a sweet and melancholy character who embodies the city's reticent poetry. Milan's *Donnina* is a statue that De Biasi has pursued for fourteen years, going to photograph her in all seasons, impelled by a mysterious sixth sense. When he published a book about this secret companion, it was discovered that she was a work of Marino Marini. They had put her on top of the Montestella, a hill built up over the years by rubbish. When her illustrious origins were revealed, the little lady was transferred to the noble setting of the gardens.

In the fabulous Villa Invernizzi gardens in the Via Cauppuccini, proud flamingoes glide along the paths (photo 151). A rare vision of Africa in Milan, the kingdom of a solitary prince in the midst of the forest. It gives the lie forever to the myth that Milan is a city without surprises, without its own poetic enigma.

An extremely elegant composition with sober elements; a crescendo from wood to stone; from columns to a riot of vegetation; from vases to cupids; making the atmosphere of a seventeenth century cloister in the Via San Martino (photo 152), as composed as any painting. Then leaving this classical vision, we come to the subtle shudder that De Chirico's pool gives us in the park in front of the *Triennale* (photo 153). It is mid-winter and the snow, with its slightly spectral reflections, has created a play of illusionist magic issuing from the artist's imagination around the swan and the human figures.

The overhanging trees in the park, the white stains of the snowy stretch and the solitary statues create the atmosphere of a brooding nightmare in which anything is possible. From here it is easy to step into a fairy tale Milan with ducks sliding into a regimented acquatic «armada» on the lake while the Castle (photo 154) watches through the fog in the background. This is the surprising Milan of inner voices, the city that hides its secrets. It is a northern world that Milan reveals only in Winter. For that reason, when he was asked to do a book on Milan in the space of a few months, De Biasi asked for a full twelve months. «I want to have a full year at my disposal», he explained, «in order to represent all the seasons: because there is a different Milan in each season». The seaside sunniness of Milan's *Idroscalo* corresponds to the indefinite, stealthy, romantic, northern atmosphere of Autumn. Here there is a Californian vision with the *Resegone* sparkling in the background (photo 155) and with a canoe's splash of yellow colour (photo 156). The enchantment of America's canoeing country is repeated in front of the Sforza castle already seen in the romantic, yearning atmosphere of English poetry. Milan is thus capable of infinite metamorphosis.

146

147

148

150

151

155

156

158

159

The springs of Milan

As far as fountains go, Milan is not Rome. Milan does not have that incredible wealth of fountains that led Respighi to set those of the capital to music. But even so, Milan's fountains do suggest a poetic vein that characterizes the unique city.

A cherub watches the water happily spurting in a private garden in the Via Manzoni (photo 164). All around is a symphony of colour. The vitality of Milanese fountains lies in their spreading around themselves an image of joyousness only scarcely touched by melancholy. At times they appear in the guise of a severe and secretive old timer like the fountain at the Central Station. Or else as the traditional fountains that filled the city in the past (photo 164). Some of them overlook almost Florentine scenes, such as here in the Via Romagnosi in front of the Cassa di Risparmio (photo 165). The pure concept of the Milanese fountain was not spared the monumentalism of the nineteen thirties. Here is an extraordinary glimpse of one of the most typical and most beautiful, located in a house built in the architectural style of the Fascist regime in the nineteen thirties. The muscular colossus representing «Roman-ness» stretches out to observe the blue play of clean water while the figures below give a sense of monumental proportion to the composition.

The fountain in photo 162 is a Fascist fountain that communicates an impression of an unusual vigour of proportion and reveals an ardour of composition that evokes admiration.

And here inside the Sforza castle is the fountain with the classic dragon motif (photo 167). Like everything inscribed within this solemn Renaissance architecture, it shows that elegance of outline and the continuous and intense rhythm that goes beeneath the surface. Here and in the wonderful image of the fountain in photo 169 we are in the realm of classic proportion, seeking a prototype of aetherial simplicity. But even in this case, we often find outselves confronted by elaborate images of an almost Baroque richness. The fountain in Via Romagnosi (photo 169) is very amusing with its muddle of picturesque elements and its exaggerated theatricality. And the goddess in Piazza Fontana covered with droplets of water (photo 170) symbolizes a calm monumentality, the meditative pathos characteristic of Milanese art.

But a certain subtle humour always blossoms, too. It is said that Milan has remained a «Gothic» city. And here is one of the Gothic creatures par excellence, the frog, constituting the attraction of the little fountain in the cloister of Santa Maria delle Grazie (photo 171). The Milanese bestiary is rich and varied. Amid the Duomo's statuary population, in the courtyards and in the palaces, in frescoes and tapestries, emerge animals of every sort: from the classic Visconti dragon to frog, unicorns and even a malicious cat.

The fountains, too, add to this magical imaginary zoo in which the strangest animals acquire a surprisingly Milanese appearance.

Then one jumps from the city's romantic clouds right into futuristic Milan's incredible precision. The lens has captured the fountain in an ultra-modern kindergarten building. With an elegant play of volumes, the green fountain (photo 172) is inserted like a sculpture into the impressive geometry of an abstact painting. Here is the courageous adventure of twentieth century art: the will to make anew and to make beautiful, to want to, always, even if there is the danger of being wrong. The generous concept of Massimo Bontempelli comes to mind when he recommended artists to «... always take off, even at the risk of breaking your necks after a minute...», and he added, «How can a new architecture rise if it doesn't rouse enthusiasm and if it doesn't exaggerate?». These reflections come to mind after looking at the daring and the excessive joy of certain Milanese fountains.

The fountains have also become part of the city's mythology as places for meeting and even as places for cures with almost prodogious results. The fountain of the *Acqua Marcia*, situated between the arena and the park (photo 173) is typical. Many old age pensioners use the hearby benches as a meeting place. Hours pass by in serenity and nostalgia. Then they take home water from the fountain for its medicinal properties. Another enchanting touch of the old, unpredictable city.

And in the Piazzale Giulio Cesare you encounter a jet of water and an exultation of flowers (photo 174).

The statue's headgear is confused with the white policeman's helmet: an image that is an integral part of the Milanese scene. Humour and yearning wed in a delightful picture.

163

164

165

167

168

169

170

171

172

The people

Milan is a big city, particularly for its inhabitants. A people of an extraordinary flexibility and of unique characterstics combined with a native humour. Introversion tempered by outbursts of humour; an always lively, practical imagination; a fluctuation between joy and the tempest; an extremely restless humanity. De Biasi has captured a series of scenes illustrating the Milanese character.

A woman lingering in the Piazza del Duomo (photo 175) confides her problems to a policemen. The «cop» is one of Milan's best-loved institutions. The traditional, slightly odious face of authority is diluted in this figure of firmly popular character. The policeman is seen as a friend, as a Milanese in uniform. The popular imagination always invests him with a congenial nature. The two gigantic policemen with handsome beards and reddish moustaches standing guard at the entrance to the Palazzo Marino, Milan's town hall, were popularly dubbed «the Bronzes of Riace». And here are a variety of actors. The craftsman-antique dealer who stands outside his shop in the Via Lanzone, in hidden Milan (photo 176). A leer with a wink, the typically Milanese sparkling eyes, the cigarette casually dangling from the corner of his mouth gives him the look of the Naviglio's Jean Gabin. Then here is a curious character in the Via Paolo Sarpi playing with a monkey who essays an ironic kiss at the Spring Fair (photo 178). A happy, colourful scene that seems to be taking place at the Portobello market in London.

The protagonist is an eccentric with garish tie and checked suit, but the Milanese quality is saved by the sarcastic pace of the whole. One finds the Parisian-style vitality of Milan in the artist fallen asleep while showing his paintings at the Naviglio fair (photo 178). A poetic, slightly anachronistic figure taken from a gathering of surrealist painters or from a René Clair film. These, too, belong to the *féerie*, the myth of the Milanese world balanced between the solidity of industry and a lyrical folly. It is no accident that *la vie boheme* blossomed here, just at the moment when the great Milan of capitalism burst on the scene. In a few years the relationship will be measured between the Milan of the nineteen sixties throbbing with the economic miracle, the great immigration, the banks and quick fortunes, and the artistic climate of the Brera: the painters Dova, Crippa and Fontana, the growth of artistic ambitions and the breakdown of surroundings like that described in that great film panorama, Antonioni's *La Notte*. It is no accident that Milan has become the capital of fashion and a centre for artists of great taste like Armani, Missoni and Versace. There is always a lively fermentation of dream reality with a profound underpinning of imagery.

It is also a human enough city, rooted in simple tastes and traditions. Here is the *bocce* festival (photo 179): a spontaneous gaiety that can be found in neighbourhood festivities; in the Stramilano dancing and markets. Carnival may be less typical here than in other cities like Venice, but here it lasts longer than in any other Italian city. It is a carnival of strong and slightly enigmatic colours (photo 180-181); two-sided like so many of the metropolis' manifestations. In the anxious years bridging the seventies and eighties, when Milan was shaken by terrorism and criminal violence, the Carnival often assumed contradictory and paradoxical aspects. The masks in their ambiguity seemed to reflect the uncertainties that gripped the city. The violence of the colours, always a characteristic of the Milanese Carnival, reflected then the frightening violence outside.

This photograph (photo 182) taken in Carnival time is perhaps the image that best renders the secret of popular Milan's animation. A downpour of confetti has invaded the church square and a population of festive ants runs wild in waves of colour. Here one can sense the allegory of Milan as a perpetual moveable feast, as a delirium of motion and continual transformation. A city that unceasingly grows out of itself and presents itself in a thousand different ways. There is a Parisian atmosphere: the Brera as *quartier latin* (photo 183) where there alternate mannequins' plastic breasts, second-hand typewriter frames and the American Stars and Stripes. And there is the traditional, popular image of the *cadreghe-umbrellat,* the craftsman who mends chairs and sells umbrellas near the sumptuous Palazzo Litta. These are the personalities that propagate the Milanese spirit, from whom emanate that subtle *malaise* of the Gallery, described by Giuseppe Marotta.

Sporting Milan is an epic tale apart with its teams representing a category, a state of being, a landscape of the soul. *Inter,* the image and portrait of a solid bourgeoisie, delightfully arrogant, the expression of the world of the ambitious, of office workers and of the more up-to-date working classes.The popular Giuseppe Meazza, nicknamed «Balilla» in the Fascist era and Lorenzi, the smiling «Veleno» of the post-war period, were its symbols. Then there is *Milan* whose poets and chroniclers have described it as the team of despair and of dreams, of boundless romanticism and of a Milanese bohemianism. Realistic *Inter;* romantic and poetic *Milan* - the city's two faces.

Milan introduced a nordic air with its wonderworking trio, Gre-No-Li: Gren, Nordhal and Liedholm, the Wagnerian poets of football's flight of the Valkyries. And *Inter* with Nyers, «*le grand Etienne,*» a Hungarian rich in verve who symbolized the passions of a Gothic city. This aspect should not be undervalued in a city that celebrates its most straightforward public holiday on Sundays in the stadium (photo 185). From my point of view, it is profoundly significant that the people go to celebrate that other popular festival, the famous Stramilano parade wearing armour signed by the great stylist Missoni (photo 186).

Fantasy and art, popularity and style follow one another and are entangled in this saga of Paris on the Lambro.

De Biasi now takes us flying over the Duomo (photo 188) like the dreaming tramps in

Zavattini and De Sica's famous *Miracolo a Milano* of 1950. Here are two young lovers dazzled by the crowd of statues. They represent hope, the individual and collective dream, and they are ravished and in ecstasy, enchanted by a timeless Milan. Going up on to the Duomo's roof is a classical Milanese pastime. «It's worth the money,» they say when they've reached the top. «From below you can't see how amazing Milan is.» And in fact the surprising aspects are continuous. De Biasi plays with irony, designing a curious composition where the people's legs echo those on the poster above them (photo 188). And another surprising play on fantasy was suggested by the fashion poster in photo 189. He photographed it eight times yet was still not content. He could not get the sophisticated atmosphere right. In the end, as in a revelation, he saw four young girls passing by and he caught the dialogue between them and the figures in the poster. Milan is the disembarkation point for all fashion and for all dreams. A Nordic tourist in an incredible hat has stopped in the Brera's courtyard to takes notes. Suddenly even she is part of the Milanese atmosphere, an insertion in the more solemn moments of history (photo 190).

The Milanese is happy when he can mix with his equals to animate the varied picture of collective life. He bends curiously over the curiosites of the Senigallia Fair, his flea market: the Ambrosian Portobello road (photo 191). And every year the Via Bargutta is enlivened with painters displaying their work in the open – a feast of art in the swarming street (photo 192). Milan welcomes and understands everyone: the great artist or the Sunday painter who captures the trees' transparent luminosity in the park (photo 193). Sport and art; life and dream; beauty and colour – this is the Milan that goes from joy to happiness always adding new touches to a face never wholly exposed. A frenzy of colourful jerseys worn by the bicycle-riding participants in the Stramilano (photo 194) while greens and blues predominate in the parade of majorettes down Via Paolo Sarpi during the Grape Festival (photo 195).

In the course of his photo reportage, De Biasi nervously asked himself how to discuss work in Milan. Work is one of the fundamental aspects of the people's life and in Milan, it is a story charged with complexity and reflected in a thousand facets. Alfa Romeo, Pirelli, Motta: how can they be described? De Biasi chose to describe the Milan-Tokyo: the commuters' daily arrival in the city (photo 196). The arrival of the commuter trains in the Metropolis means factories, tires, motorcycles and cars. And here is a vision of the Porta Romana station when the 7:39 comes in from Piacenza. Commuters arrive at every point: at Bovisa, at Lambrate, at the North station and at Porta Genova. These morning crowds make up the mosaic of the great working Milan. Together in the fever of arrival come the labourer, the white collar worker, the designer, the mechanic and the gladiators of the third class from the changing metropolis. A railway station recounts all these things. O Railroads, I hear your heart. And at the end of the chapter on people, here is a symbolic enough photograph (photo 197) recapitulating a great deal of the discussion about the city. We are on the Porta Garibaldi bridge and the figure of a Franciscan Friar stands out against the outline of the Hotel Executive's glass wall: brown and alone in the noise of the city. The powerful presence of the future and solitary meditation; Faith and Progress; man and the grandeur of technology and architecture. Milan tempers contrast; it dilutes the strident elements; and seeks to mitigate man's cry of pain. The ancient heart of the city is perhaps on the side of the Friar suffering and dreaming alone.

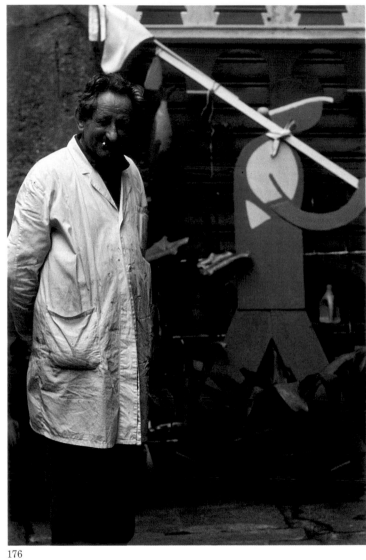

176

177

178

180

181

185

186

191

192

194

195

The fascination of the colour

The festive variety of colours is also one of the characteristics of Milan, often wrongly described as a grey, monochrome city. In reality there is a festive wealth of hue. The architect Mari's «loaves» (photo 198) stand between the castle and the park, a typical curiosity of the Milanese world. They have a happy resonance of colour and their bright greens, blues, oranges and violets make lively propaganda for the city. They are warming and congenial, suddenly coming down in front of your eyes, making the conquest of the metropolis a happy thing.

But the opportunities for colour in Milan are, unexpectedly infinite. Here is an unusual spectacle on the Viale Filippetti (photo 199). One morning after a rainy day, the photographer, saw the picture he had always had in mind; he had noticed it, years before, on his way to Mondadori's: cars covered with a carpet of flowers.

A pink cloud, shaken by the showers, had descended from the trees to the pavement and onto the automobiles. And the lens indulged in lovingly carressing the rain of petals and the shading off of the colours (photo 200). But the world of pink is general in Milan. A gentle carpet of this soft colour has invaded a garden behind Via Maria Pagano and the trees' imposing foilage seems to partake of it in amazement (photo 201). Yellow is also present along the edges of the streets in strange tonalities (photo 202) and also in the canary yellow song of the taxicabs (photo 203). They spread a great splash of colour in the shadow of immense palaces; in the background the Duomo's *Madonnina* spies over them. The taxis were once black and green: now they have become yellow like New York's and they give the city an imprint of festive colour. De Biasi caught one of them circling in front of the Babylonian Central Station during a quiet hour (photo 204). The giant yellow snake unwinding at the foot of mamouth walls creates a rather unusual effect. Even this suggests the lively rhythms of a great city.

The photographer began at a certain point, a systematic exploration of the city in search of red. He wanted to discover the explosive effect of this colour in a world traditionally devoted to more muffled hues. In the heart of the Naviglio, there is a beautiful red door belonging to «Mariett el Curnisatt del Navili». A slap of colour for the joy of his clients (photo 205).

But the most vertiginous symphonies of red are found on the Palazzo dei Congressi (photo 206-207) where a scarlet intoxication is wed to a festive geometry of steel tubing. And the violently intense red is once more repeated in a network of super-modern structures of the Trade Fair. Red, here, signifies igniting the imagination; a propensity for the future; disembarkation on the shores of the year 2000. Red Milan is indeed an odd fantasy: a hard sound shattering, melting and almost turning to water. It is amazing how the impact of a colour can change life's proportions. But this Milan is extremely enigmatic: it has a ripe persimmon's explosive colour.

Its joyful yet desperate words hang in the air like a feather. We thought we understood everything about Milan, yet seeing it now transposed to a colour code has upset both ideas and sensations. However, red does signify a victory of life.

Blue instead, in the windows or on the walls of a gallery (photo 208-209), makes us fall into disquieting undersea abysses. Here resounds the secret chord of a nervous and furiously creative Milan.

The same note that has sponsored so many political and artistic novelties in the twentieth century: from Fascism to Futurism, from the Center-Left to avant-guard design. In order to recover the sumptuous Milan of the past, however, one must linger over its golden statues (photo 211-212).

These give the measure of another aspect of fantasy: the lavish and the astonishing. The city never tires of amazing us with its multiplicity. And its own symbol, the *Madonnina*, is a golden reflection in the night (photo 213). But here we are dealing with a copy that shines on top of the Pirelli building. This introduces an anecdote that explains the Milanese character quite well. When the Pirelli skyscraper was built, the city's inhabitants said, «Up until now the Duomo's spire was the highest point in Milan and from its height, the statue-symbol protected our metropolis. Now that the highest point is atop the Pirelli building, it's only right that the *Madonnina* should go there». And a copy of the familiar statue was placed up there to protect Milan and its fantastc colours.

199

200

205

206

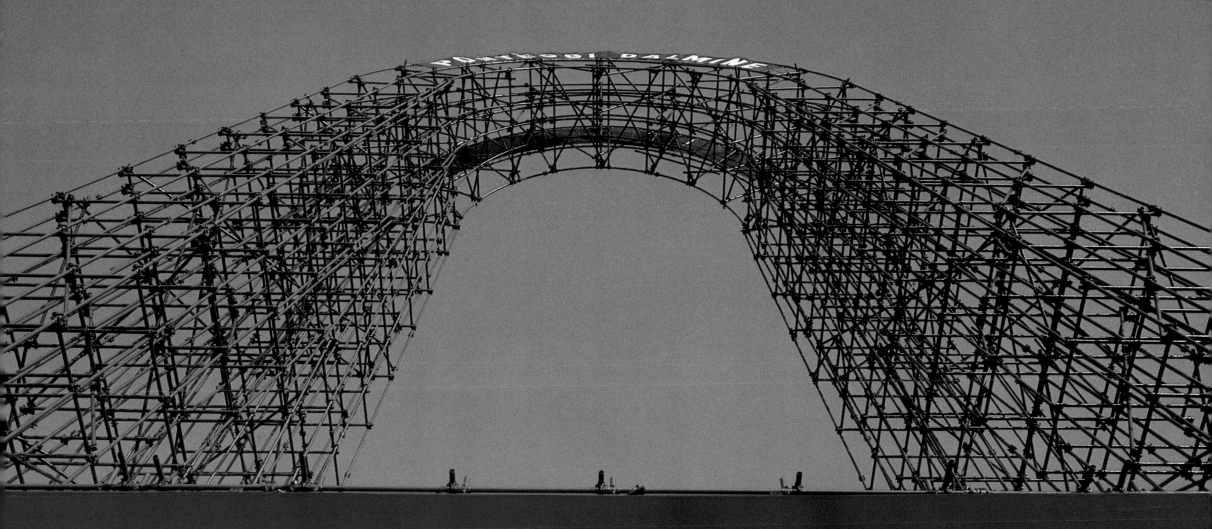

ATM

scuolaintram

SERVIZIO
SPECIALE

1927

209

210

211

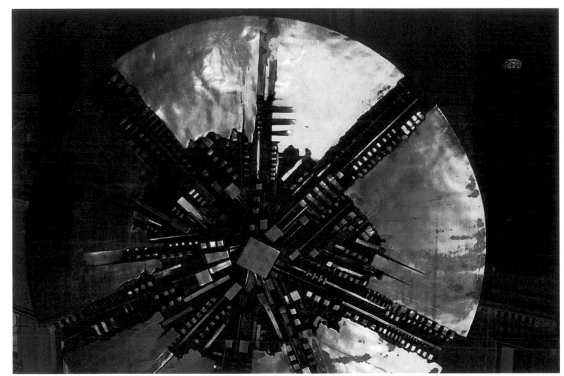

212

The Naviglio canals

With the Naviglio's canals, although we find ourselves still in a classically Milanese world, we leave Milan in a certain sense. We penetrate the world of pure fantasy, in the Ticino's *quai des brumes*, in a foggy harbour that evokes the fantasies of Pierre McOrlan, of Francis Carco, of Simenon obliging us to immerse ourselves in a subtly French atmosphere. Even though some English guide books describe the characteristic Vicolo delle Lavandaie in the Naviglio as one of the most typically characteristic places in the Lombard metropolis, this is undoubtedly one of the most European and international areas of Milan. Here Milan loses completely those homely, peasant touches that tend to restrict vision. Here Milan becomes a place of air fantasy, a landscape and country of the soul. The Vicolo delle Lavandaie is a national monument. And in their way, so too are the courtyards that represent the last possible refuge of a bohemian life for painters. So too are the characteristic inns with their gardens and the *bateaux mouches* that tour the Naviglio showing off the beauty of secret waterways and the beauty of secret byways like those of Paris at its most brilliant. The Naviglio festival is one of the classical popular gatherings in the city and recalls France's Bastille Day street dancing or else the film *Casco d'Oro* with the splendid Simonne Signoret. Every last Sunday of the month, there is an antiques fair: a brilliant, Parisian style affair, always full of fresh imagination.

The Naviglio of Milan is more or less a memory. It represented a great network of navigation already in existence in the late Middle Ages, then splendidly improved under the Visconti and the Sforza and brought to completion with the ingenious innovations of Leonardo da Vinci. The centre of the system is still the *Darsena*, a small lake located between the inner walls (Viale D'Annunzio) and the outer walls (Viale Gorizia) of the city. Once upon a time, barge loads of sand were brought to this setting of an extraordinarily anguished, natural poetry.

Many artists and *Litterateurs* (Elio Vittorini among others), obliged to live in Milan, chose to settle here in order to imbibe the vivid odour of time.

De Biasi has purposefully chosen to photograph the *Darsena* in mid-Winter with the snow and the light reflecting steely winter transparencies. Vapours rise from the lake (photo 215) because the water is warmer than the air. Thus the surface exhales its warm breath. In the background lies a typical Naviglio landscape. A bit Kafkaesque, with black houses waiting in ambush, bell towers, bridges and the eyes of mangled windows. The Naviglio people are characterized by a strong sense of communication. They are frequently extravagent types: artists and adventurers, uprooted, seeking for something. Their temperament is reflected in the life of the quarter. Little meeting places mushroom there: piano-bars, night spots, cafés that resemble those of a Milanese Montparnasse. Here is a tasteful «Conversation Place» (photo 217) whose very name attracts those looking for human contact. Certainly the Naviglio houses a peculiar bohemian fauna, but the atmosphere is one of sincerity and an extremely anti-conformist style of life. Milan here shows us the hidden side of the moon. A poetic and looney metropolis, far from the world of computers and company rules and regulations, far from the time clocks and shirtsleeves that occupy much of its scene elsewhere. Here the imagination is unleashed in its most fruitful fashion and the artists' vivacity establishes freer relationships with reality.

A walk along the Naviglio encourages falling in love with a completely unknown Milan. Under the bridge of the Alzaia Naviglio Grande (photo 218) there appear multiple reflections: trees, colours of cars, houses, creating a Venetian kind of setting. And something of Venice is suggested in the images of the Naviglio festival (photo 219) when the people throng the quarter and unusually shaped boats slip over the water. It is a rather typical, popular entertainment with games, booths, open air kitchens. It is characterized by the participation of young people in the human dimension of the landscape and in the setting's anti-conformity. The other side of the coin of capitalist and corportate Milan: a plunge into life's primitive simplicity with a pinch of bohemianism, of Parisian Apaches or the *On the Road* spirit of America in the sixties.

The Naviglio is a paradise of painters. One of these (photo 220) has painted and hung up on a wall his own «Vicolo delle Lavandaie». De Biasi has thus captured this classic scene, not with a direct image that might seem a bit trite, but in this slightly naive transposition provided by this son of the quarter.

The difference between these images and those of the Milan that we have seen on the preceeding pages, for all their highly personal originality, is an enormous one. And this underlines the fact that the Naviglio is a reality of its own. It is an island of art and fantasy in the heart of the modern metropolis. Look at the poetic tenderness of the images in this completely painted courtyard (photo 222).

The paintings are as clear and clean as if they were hung inside a palace swept and tidied up daily. The colours are festive and at the same time restful. The fresh imagination in this tenement evokes a limitless succession of terraces, balconies, window boxes, dormers, projections and constructions overlaid and inserted into one another. Everywhere Milan is beautiful, but here the imagination is awakened and plays strange tricks.

Here are the curiosities of the antiques show that is held once a month on Sunday. Small, neatly made tables; wash basins; black masks of rough Picasso faces; pans; teapots; coloured lamps; rare copper (photo 223-226). The variety of the objects is reflected in the Naviglio's mocking waters. The sensation of being in a singular place is complete. The Naviglio is a playful chaos of bodies, of dreams, of guts, tripe, viscera and human limbs as if the population of Milan were remade into a single body and a committee of savage, delirious surgeons amused themselves by cutting it up and taking out stones, streets, courtyards, wrought iron, statues, smiles and grimaces of equal intensity.

The pleasure of an excursion on the Naviglio is complete with a breath of fresh lake air (photo 227-229). Here are the famous swimming and boating schools. During the holidays, the *Darsena* and the Naviglio witness an extraordinary blossoming of boats getting ready to race. Thus Milan, in happy colours, indulges itself in the maritime dreams of its inhabitants.

«If only there were the sea at Milan...» as Dino Buzzati wrote. We have reached the end of our pilgrimage to the heart of a fascinating and unusual Milan (photo 230). The joyful Christmas illuminations greet the Naviglio festivities. Large festoons stretch over the waters, sparkling and teeming with golden light. Milan in this fantastic sunset is more elusive and magic than ever. We have pursued it over its pavements and into its courtyards, in the palaces and churches, amid the people and on the Naviglio, only to feel ourselves vanquished by its poetic uncommunicativeness as in an Antonioni film. Milan is a sphynx and a siren, an enigma wrapped in its mystery. The most beautiful city in the world, Stendhal said, for those who know how to penetrate the dark silence of its byways and lose themselves there as if for ever.

216

223

224

225

227

228

Printed by Grafiche Lema of Maniago/Pordenone
in the month of November 1984

Graphic design:
Armando e Maurizio Milani / Milan-New York

Consultant for photolithography and printing:
Enrico Mazzoli

Photolithography:
Graphicolor / Milan